⇧ Luftwaffe IDS seen with a full compliment of fuel tanks

First produced in 2009 by SAM Limited, under licence from SAM Publications
Media House, 21 Kingsway, Bedford, MK42 9BJ, United Kingdom

ISBN 978-1-906959-01-2

Typeset by SAM Limited, Media House, 21 Kingsway, Bedford, MK42 9BJ, UK
Designed by Simon Sugarhood
Printed and bound in the United Kingdom by Buxton Press, United Kingdom

Author's Note
Whilst every care has been taken in the gathering of images for this book, either
from original sources, via third party collections or the author's own archives, every
effort has been made to identify and credit photographers responsible for the
photograph and where possible obtain the necessary permissions for their use.
However the publishers cannot accept responsibility for any omissions beyond
their control and should any persons feel their copyright has been inadvertently
breached, please contact the author via the publisher.

Acknowledgments
Thanks are due to the following for their assistance with information and
photographs that populate this publication: Michael Ullman; Des Brennan; Mike
Tomlinson; RAF Media Relations and BAe Systems Press Office.

Andy Evans
February 2009

Chapter 1

Tornado Origins

⇧ Tornado P.02 XX946 taxies out

The Panavia Tornado was a joint development by the United Kingdom, West Germany and Italy for a high-speed, low-level interdictor/strike aircraft, and now as a mature aircraft the Tornado remains one of the world's most sophisticated and able attack aircraft, capable of carrying a large payload, endowed with long range and high survivability.

The Tornado was developed and built by Panavia, a tri-national consortium consisting of BAe Systems, MBB of Germany and Alenia Aeronautica of Italy. During the 1960s, aeronautical designers looked to variable geometry designs to gain the manoeuvrability and efficient cruise of straight wings with the speed of swept-wing designs. Britain and France initiated the AFVG (Anglo French Variable Geometry)

⇧ Prototype P.01/D-9591 undertaking ground running tests – note the mesh covers on the intakes

⇧ Prototype P.03/XX947 the first Tornado with dual controls. It was also the first Tornado to be delivered in camouflage and the first with a radome rather than a representative fairing

project in 1965, which ended with French withdrawal in 1967, however in 1968 West Germany, the Netherlands, Belgium, Italy, and Canada formed a working group to examine replacements for the F-104 Starfighter, initially called the Multi Role Aircraft (MRA), and later the Multi Role Combat Aircraft (MRCA). Britain joined the MRCA group in 1968, and a memorandum of agreement was drafted between Britain, West Germany, and Italy or as one RAF source of the time commented – MRCA - 'Must Refurbish Canberra Again'!

The programme was intended to produce a single-seat replacement for the F-104G for Germany and a two-seat strike fighter for Britain and Italy. Canada and Belgium pulled out in 1969; however the four remaining partner nations - United Kingdom, Germany, Italy, and the Netherlands, formed Panavia Aircraft GmbH on 26 March 1969, although the Netherlands pulled out in 1970. The United Kingdom and West Germany each had a 42.5% stake, with the remaining 15% going to Italy. The production share was also agreed upon - the front fuselage and tail assembly in the United Kingdom, the centre fuselage in West Germany, and the wings in Italy. A separate multinational company, Turbo Union, was formed in June 1970 to develop and build the RB199 engines for the aircraft, with ownership similarly split 40% Rolls-Royce, 40% MTU, and 20% FIAT.

At the conclusion of the project definition phase in May 1970, the concepts were reduced to two designs: a single-seat Panavia 100 for West Germany, and the twin-seat Panavia 200 which the RAF preferred and which would eventually become the Tornado. In September 1971 the three governments signed an Intention to Proceed (ITP)

document. The RAF subsequently decided that it needed an air defence fighter, and initiated the separate development of the Tornado ADV. The contract for the Batch 1 aircraft was signed on 29 July 1976 and the first aircraft were delivered to the RAF and Luftwaffe on 5 and 6 June 1979 respectively, whereas the first Italian Tornado was delivered on 25 September 1981. On 29 January 1981 the Tri-national Tornado Training Establishment (TTTE) officially opened at RAF Cottesmore to train pilots and navigators from all three nations on the new aircraft. Production ended in 1998 after some 992 aircraft of all variants had been built for the three partner nations, and the last aircraft to be completed was for the Royal Saudi Air Force, the sole export customer.

Chapter 2

RAF Tornado GR.1

For the RAF the Tornado was designed for ultra-low-level penetration strikes on Warsaw Pact targets in Europe using both conventional and tactical nuclear weapons, such as the WE.177. However the end of the Cold War thankfully precluded such weapons from ever seeing use. The aircraft also needed to be capable of taking off and landing in short distances from airfields that were considered to be vulnerable to aerial attack. To aid this thrust reversers were fitted and contribute to one of the aircraft's traits – the appearance of soot on the fin surface. The cockpit is of conventional design with a centre stick and left hand throttles and multi-function displays for both the pilot and navigator. Perhaps the major feature of the Tornado is its terrain following radar, which allows for all-weather hands-off low-level flight. The RAF Tornadoes also have the unique Laser Ranger and Marked Target Seeker (LRMTS) under the fuselage on the starboard side, in an aerodynamic fairing. This system can be used to

⇧ Tri-National Tornadoes. A formation of Cottesmore based aircraft where all basic IDS training was undertaken

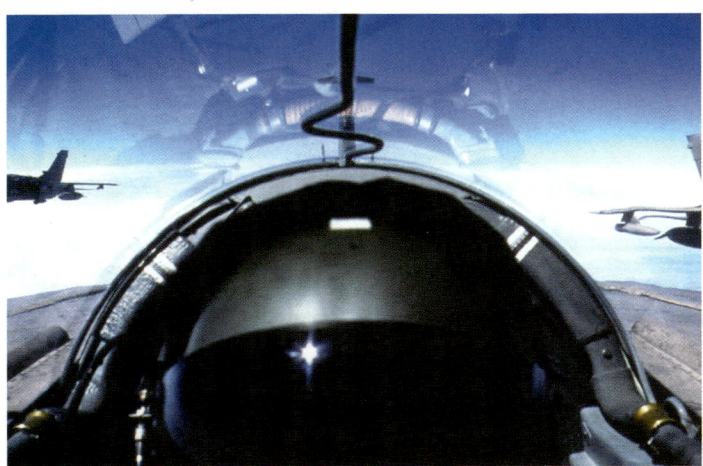

⇧ A Tornado GR.1 formation – seen from the back seat

measure the slant range of a point on the ground relative to the aircraft. This information is then used by the avionics to compute targeting information for the crew. The LRMTS can also be used to receive reflected laser energy from a third-party laser, allowing the crew to find targets that have been marked by troops on the ground or by another aircraft.

For the RAF the Tornado GR.1 was the first generation version of the strike aircraft with some 228 examples ordered, the first being delivered on June 5, 1979 and entering service in the early 1980s. The main differences between British, German and Italian IDS aircraft lie in the individual user nation's choice of avionics equipment, and uniquely, all RAF GR.1s had an extra 121 gallon fuel tank in their tail fins, giving the aircraft an additional internal fuel capacity. Bolt-on IFR probes were also introduced on some of the RAF machines; although this was not a common sight

⇧ ZA599 gets airborne from RAF Honington

⇧ A pre-production Tornado get airborne

⇧ Tornado in flight – seen from the back seat

⇧ ZD711 banks away giving a great view of the GR.1's underside

⇧ ZA599 of the RAF's Tactical Weapons Conversion Unit – TWCU

⇧ Note the early style of three-tone camouflage here

⇧ Seen from the back seat, a No.XV Squadron Tornado

⇧ ZA368 of No.45(R) Squadron of the RAF's Tactical Weapons Conversion Unit

⇧ A No.XV Squadron GR.1

⇧ A GR.1 from No.617 Squadron in Gulf colours – note the code letters – reflecting those of the Dam Busters Lancaster's of WWII

⇧ One of the 'Gold Stars' of No.31 Squadron

⇧ A line-up of Tornado GR.1s prior to Operation Desert Fox

⇧ Going to low-level – the Tornado GR.1's raison-d'être!

⇧ The Tornado's nose swung to one side reveals the avionics

on the Germany-based aircraft, they were useful for the UK-stationed Tornadoes, giving them additional range to strike targets in Europe should this become necessary. The main conventional weapons used by RAF Tornadoes were the Mks 1–12 500lb free-fall or parachute-retarded bombs, the latter fitted with a Hunting Mk118 retarding tail. The Mk 13-22 1,000lb bombs could be used either slick' for delivery from medium level or for lofting attacks and for low-level use, the same weapon could be fitted with a Hunting Mk 117 parachute-retarding tail. Tornado GR.1s could also carry a range of specialised munitions such as the Hunting BL755 cluster bomb, in both original and 'improved' forms, and a weapon unique to the RAF Tornado – the Hunting JP233 anti-airfield weapon. Other items included ALARM anti-radar missiles, and Paveway laser-guided bombs. The aircraft was also fitted with twin internal 27mm Mauser cannon, located below the cockpit floor.

The GR.1 aircraft were destined to equip eleven RAF front-line strike/attack/reconnaissance squadrons, with eight based in Germany. The first unit to operate the Tornado was No.9 Squadron, which received its initial aircraft, ZA586, in January 1982 and officially re-formed on the type the following June at RAF Honington. No.617 Squadron re-formed on Tornados in May 1983 at Marham, along with No.27 Squadron, (later No.12 Squadron) which reappeared in August 1983. In addition to these front-line units, a handful of Tornadoes were assigned to the Tornado Operational Evaluation Unit at Boscombe Down. With the full complement of three home-based squadrons successfully established, units in RAF Germany began to re-equip with the Tornado and a higher priority was given to the squadrons which had been operating the Buccaneer. The first to do so was No.15 Squadron, which re-formed on the Tornado at Laarbruch in October 1983 and was followed by RAF Germany's other Buccaneer unit, No.16 Squadron, in February 1984. No.20 Squadron, based at Bruggen, re-

⇧ ZA326 in the RAE's 'Raspberry Ripple' colours

⇧ A No.12 Squadron aircraft being armed with Paveway bombs

⇧ ALARM missiles being loaded aboard a GR.1

⇧ Low intensity formation lights were trialled but not adopted

⇧ The TIALD pod

⇧ 1999 saw further action for the GR.1s in the Balkans when aircraft from RAF Bruggen took part in the conflict

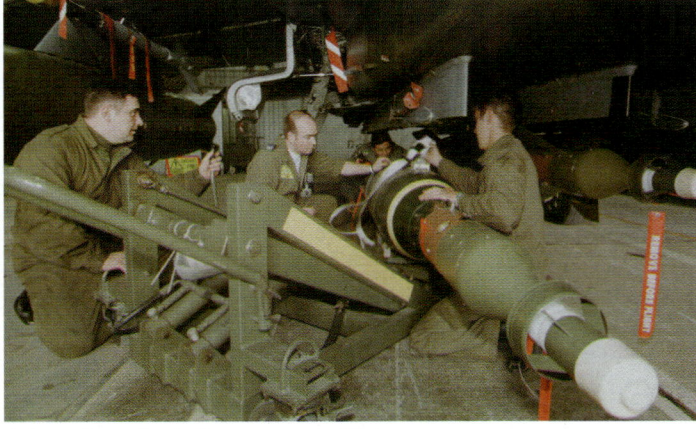
⇧ Ground crew load a Paveway onto a GR.1

⇧ ZD851 with practice bombs aboard

⇧ Taxiing out on an Operation Bolton strike mission

⇧ A No.IX Squadron GR.1 with ALARM anti-radar missiles fitted

⇧ A No.617 Squadron GR.1

⇧ A No.14 Squadron GR.1

⇧ A No.IX Squadron GR.1

⇧ A No.17 Squadron GR.1

equipped in June 1984, also at Laarbruch and No.31 Squadron stood-up at Bruggen in November 1984, whilst two other squadrons converted to the Tornado from the Jaguar during 1985, these being No.17 and No.14. A total of 228 GR.1s were built for the RAF, thirty-six of these being dual control and designated GR1(T).

The GR.1's combat debut came in 1991 during the Gulf War when aircraft were deployed to airbases at Muharraq, Tabuk and Dhahran. In the early stages of the conflict Tornadoes were used to target Iraqi military airfields using JP233's. Operations later switched to medium level, later using Laser Guided Bombs. In the aftermath of the war a number of Tornadoes remained in the Gulf based at Ali Al Salem in Kuwait for operations over the Southern No Fly Zone under the aegis of 'Operation Bolton'. GR.1s later took part in 'Operation Desert Fox' in 1998 following more intransigence from the Iraqi leadership. 1999 saw further action for the GR.1s in the Balkans conflict when aircraft from RAF Bruggen in Germany were involved in the first phase of the war flying precision strike missions. They later moved to Corsica shortly before the war ended in order to bring them closer to the combat zone. Following the Kosovo War, the GR.1 was phased with aircraft being upgraded to the GR.4 standard. The final GR.1/4 upgrade was delivered to the RAF in 2003.

Chapter 3
Tornado GR.1A/GR.4A

GR.1A was a reconnaissance variant of the Tornado GR.1 RAF and with the upgrade of the GR.1 to GR.4 standard, similarly the GR.1A became the GR.4A. The GR.1A was equipped with the internally mounted TIRRS (Tornado Infra-Red Reconnaissance System), one on each side of the fuselage and a single IRLS (Infra-Red Linescan) reconnaissance sensor mounted on the underside of the fuselage. The sensor package replaced the 27 mm cannon and unlike most reconnaissance packages which store their images on 35mm film or similar, the GR.1A used video tape to save information. In all the RAF ordered thirty airframes, either as rebuilds of GR.1s or as new airframes, and 25 aircraft were later upgraded to GR.4A standard.

As noted, at the heart of the GR.1A's abilities was the 'TIRRS' (Tornado Infra-Red Reconnaissance System), which consisted of three sensors, recording equipment and cockpit controls. The primary sensor was the Vinten Type 4000 IRLS

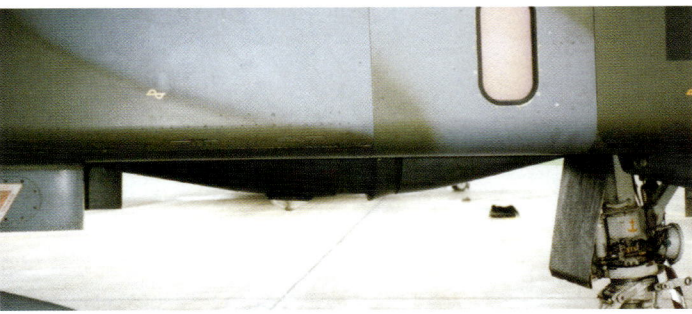

⇧ The primary sensor was the Vinten Type 4000 IRLS (Infra-Red Line Scan), mounted in a blister on the underside of the fuselage. This was a panoramic sensor with horizon-to-horizon coverage, its 'window' being a slit aperture in the underside, which had an air baffle and a protective cover when not in use

⇧ A GR.1A with full wing sweep taken during Operation Granby

(Infra-Red Line Scan), mounted in a blister on the underside of the fuselage. This was a panoramic sensor with horizon-to-horizon coverage, its 'window' being a slit aperture in the underside, which had an air baffle and a protective cover when not in use. Complementing the IRLS were two SLIR (Side Looking Infra-Red) sensors mounted either side of the forward fuselage. The SLIRs have a field of view from the horizon down to 10-degree depression, and are used to fill in the image close to the horizon in better detail than is possible with IRLS. Imagery was produced by an EO

⇧ Complementing the IRLS were two SLIR (Side Looking Infra-Red) sensors mounted either side of the forward fuselage

⇧ Note the IRLS (Infra-Red Linescan) reconnaissance sensor mounted on the underside of the fuselage

⇧ During the Gulf War the GR.1A was introduced to the RAF fleet and undertook Scud Hunts

⇧ ZA401/R, a No.II(AC) Squadron GR.1A readied for a trip to the frozen wastes!

⇧ In addition to the TIRRS, the GR.IA could carry a Vicon 18 Series 601 podded sensor for situations where low-level operations are precluded

⇧ A No.II(AC) GR.1A seen at low level over the North Sea. The TIRRS was an ideal platform for low-level reconnaissance

⇧ Note the drop tanks have also received an Arctic wash

⇧ A line-up of No.13 Squadron recce jets at RAF Lossiemouth; note the aircraft on the right wears the newly introduced grey camouflage

⇧ Seen shortly after its return from Operation Telic, this No.13 Squadron recce jet still shows signs of the removal of the conflict-specific ARTF paint finish

⇧ RAPTOR (Reconnaissance Airborne Pod TORnado) was the world's first tactical day and night reconnaissance system

(electro-optical) back-plate which created a digital electric signal and transferred this to analogue video tape in real time. Each held sixty minutes of imagery, and this imagery could also be viewed on one of the navigator's 625-line TV tab screens in the rear cockpit.

In addition to the TIRRS, the GR.1A could carry a Vicon 18 Series 601 podded sensor for situations where low-level operations are precluded, rendering the TIRRS virtually useless. This contains as its primary sensor a 690 LOROP camera, shooting onto film. The main 450mm lens mounted longitudinally within a 45-degree mirror at the front reflects through 90 degrees into the camera. The main sensor window is mounted in the pod's nose cone, which allows the camera to rotate at any angle, including vertically down. In the rear of the pod is a smaller panoramic camera which provides accurate orientation of the LOROP pod's image; it has a 5in lens and uses 70mm film.

The GR.1A made its combat debut during operation 'Desert Storm' in 1991 performing admirably, bringing back the first images of a mobile Scud launcher and providing commanders with vital reconnaissance and intelligence material. By the mid 1990's however, the TIRRS was becoming increasingly expensive to operate and the wet film Vinten pod needed replacing with a modern digital system. After reviewing a number of off-the-shelf recce products, the MOD decided to have a pod purpose built for the Tornado GR.4 to be produced by the BF Goodrich Corporation in the USA. When it was introduced into RAF

⇧ GR.4A ZG713/G from No.II(AC) Squadron with RAPTOR pod fitted

⇧ The RAPTOR pod undergoing air trials work

service in 2002, the DB-110 RAPTOR (Reconnaissance Airborne Pod TORnado) was the world's first tactical day and night reconnaissance system. Similar in size to the Tornado's underwing fuel tank, the RAPTOR is an Electro-Optical and Infra-Red system with the ability to display images in the cockpit and transmit these images via a data-link to a ground station, as well as recording them in the aircraft for post-flight analysis.

The system actually made its operational debut during Operation Iraqi Freedom in early 2003 where it performed extremely well. The introduction into service of RAPTOR has allowed the RAF to withdraw the TIRRS from the Tornado and consolidate its reconnaissance exploitation assets into a single Tactical Imagery Intelligence Wing (TIW) based at RAF Marham. To this end, No.II(AC) and No.13 Squadron now fly both GR.4A and GR.4 variants as the sensors specific to the GR.4A are now not essential to the reconnaissance role.

⇧ The Vicon 18 Series 601 is seen here on a GR.4

Chapter 4
Tornado GR.1B

The GR.1B was an RAF variant designed to marry the Tornado airframe to the Sea Eagle missile in order to maintain the anti-shipping role lost with the retirement of the Buccaneer. The GR.1B was in effect no different to the standard IDS, but adapted for the maritime role and retaining all of the GR.1's avionics and weapons fits, including the FIN 1010 INS, TFR, Doppler and laser rangefinder and when the aircraft was not carrying the Sea Eagle missile it was impossible to tell them apart. Modifications were made to allow the operation of the Sea Eagle by the addition of new computer software for the modified under-fuselage shoulder pylons fitted to carry the missile. The 'Tornado In Service Maintenance Team' (TISMT) at Boscombe Down found some spare capacity in the aircraft's main computer that allowed for firing and update command lines to be wired via 'Pan Data Links' into the inboard wing and shoulder stations. Inside the rear cockpit an ex-Buccaneer Missile Control Panel was fitted to manage the Sea Eagles, and the navigator's SMS panel had the Sea Eagle firing

⇧ A No.617 Squadron Tornado GR.1B armed with two Sea Eagle missiles on modified shoulder pylon launchers

parameters added to it. The GR.1Bs were delivered in two batches from RAF St Athan, where modifications were undertaken. The Batch 1 aircraft could only 'point and shoot' the Sea Eagle and so were restricted to line-of-sight attacks only, however the Batch 2 aircraft were able to download target information into the missile's own computer and the round could be fired from a reported distance of some 110km, over the radar horizon, in 'fire-and-forget' mode, thus increasing the aircraft's survivability.

⇧ The Sea Eagle Missile

Some twenty-six former RAF Germany Batch 3 Tornadoes were converted into GR.1Bs, and the first 'Proof of Installation' aircraft, ZA409 and ZA411, were reworked at BAe Warton; being twin-stickers, they were sometimes incorrectly referred to as GR.1B(T)s. The first 'true' GR.1B, ZA407 made its first flight on 18 September 1993. The first step in the Tornado's development of a maritime role was to re-equip, Nos. 27 and 617 squadrons, with recently upgraded ex-Laarbruch GR.Is, which carried the more powerful RB.199 Mk 103 engines. The original plans called for the renumbering of No.27 Squadron, as No.12 (Designate) Squadron which, together with No.617 would move to RAF Lossiemouth in Scotland to take up the new overwater role. However, the old Buccaneer-equipped No.12 Squadron re-formed with the Tornado on 1 October 1993, the day after it stood down as a Buccaneer unit, with the unit not actually making the move north until January 1994, and No.27's numberplate being transferred to the Chinook and Puma helicopter OCU at RAF Odiham. Both Squadrons continued in this role until the retirement of the Sea Eagle missile, whereupon they reverted to their traditional duties.

⇧ The GR.1B was in effect no different to the standard IDS, but adapted for the maritime role and retaining all of the GR.1's avionics and weapons fits

Chapter 5

Tornado GR.4

⇧ One of the GR.4 development aircraft

As early as 1984 the UK Ministry of Defence began studies for a Mid-Life Update (MLU) of the Tornado fleet to rectify the shortcomings of the GR.1. This update, to Tornado GR.4 standard, would improve capability in the medium-level role while maintaining the Tornado's exceptional low-level penetration capability. The GR4 upgrade was not approved until 1994, after it had been revised to include lessons learned from the GR.1's performance in the 1991 Gulf War. One major change was the move from low-level penetration to medium-level attacks, while maintaining the low-level capability.

Some 142 Tornado GR.1s have been upgraded to GR.4 standard, under the MLU programme. The first upgraded aircraft entered service in 1998 and the GR.4 received full operational clearance in April 2001 with the final delivery taking place in June 2003, and the upgraded aircraft are planned to stay in service until 2025. The programme involved advances in systems, stealth technology and avionics whereby a digital avionics bus linked these new systems and fully integrated the aircraft's improved defensive aids suite. The weapons bus is configured to control the release of a wide range of munitions and can adapt for future weapon types through the system's missile control and weapon programming units.

The upgraded navigation systems, including a Global Positioning System (GPS), BAE Systems TERPROM digital terrain mapping system and Honeywell H-764G laser Inertial

⇧ The FLIR housing was air tested at Boscombe Down as a wooden mock-up

⇧ The final shape of the FLIR housing seen here on a No.13 Squadron jet

⇧ The LRMTS and FLIR housings are apparent here

⇧ The FLIR was developed by the Defence Research Agency and flown as a pod-mounted trials fit by the OEU at Boscombe Down

⇧ A No.13 Squadron recce jet used as a standard GR.4

⇧ Note the downward slant of the rear Brimstone missiles

⇧ A good view of the front of the GR.4 with the FLIR housing and TIALD pod

⇧ A GR.4 comes in to land carrying a RAPTOR pod

⇧ A good view of the underside of the GR.4

⇧ ALARM anti-radar missiles

⇧ A No.31 Squadron GR.4 armed with a Paveway PGM and TIALD pod

⇧ ZA462 from No.617 Squadron carrying Storm Shadow missiles

⇧ From February 2007, a number of GR.4 aircraft operating in Iraq were fitted with the Rafael Litening III targeting pod

⇧ A No.41(Reserve) Squadron aircraft from the Fast Jet and Weapons Operational Evaluation Unit with both Brimstone and TIALD fitted

⇧ Note the difference between the shape of the TIALD and Rafael Litening III pods

⇧ A superb underside view of the Storm Shadow installation

⇧ A TIALD-equipped GR.4 on finals

⇧ Firing flares from the BOZ-107 pod this LOROP-configured GR.4 shows the effectiveness of the self-protection systems

⇧ The GR.4 is fitted with a pilot's head-up display, multifunction head-down display and a digital map

Navigation System (INS) are integrated into the aircraft's main avionics system. The GR.4 is also equipped with a new Forward Looking Infrared (FLIR) housed in a fairing under the nose and opposite the LRMTS. The thermal image is projected onto the pilot's head-up and head-down displays. The addition of this feature has led to the removal of the port side Mauser cannon.

The GR.4 is further fitted with a pilot's head-up display, multifunction head-down display and a digital map. The BAe Systems TIALD Thermal Imaging Laser Designator pod, which provides high-accuracy autonomous guidance for laser-guided weapons, has been integrated on the upgraded aircraft. From February 2007, a number of GR.4 aircraft operating in Iraq were fitted with the Rafael Litening III targeting pod. The GR.4 has also been cleared to carry Enhanced Paveway II bombs, with GPS/INS (Global Positioning System/Inertial Navigation System) guidance and will also have Paveway IV in 2010. The aircraft are also now being armed with Brimstone anti-armour missiles and

⇧ The Rafael Litening III pod

⇧ Storm Shadow made its opeational debut in Operation Telic in 2003

⇧ The bright lights of Nevada as this No.41(Reserve) Squadron from the Fast Jet and Weapons Operational Evaluation Unit rests overnight before Rafael Litening III trials on the Nellis ranges

⇧ Note the unique triple launch rails of the Brimstone munition

⇧ TIALD pod on the shoulder station

⇧ Ninety-five years of 'Shiny Two'

Storm Shadow cruise missiles, the latter entering operational service in March 2003, in support of Operation Iraqi Freedom.

The GR.4 is to have a further cockpit upgrade consisting of a new Astronautics pilot's multifunction display and the BAE Systems TARDIS (Tornado Advanced Radar Display and Information System). The upgrade will enter service in 2008. The Tornado GR.4 is currently operated from two bases. Based at RAF Lossiemouth, in Scotland, are the Operational Conversion Unit, No.15(R) Squadron, and Nos.12(B), 14 and 617 Squadrons. RAF Marham is the home of the GR.4s of Nos.II(AC), IX(B), 13 and 31 Squadrons.

⇧ A No.II(AC) GR.4

⇧ A superb underfuselage shot of the Brimstone installation

RAF GR.4 Tornado

Walkaround

Photographed by Des Brennan

⇧ A low-angle view of the FLIR (right) and the LRMTS (left)

⇧ At the outset of Operation 'Telic' this head-on view shows the new FLIR and established LRMTS to good effect as well as the contour of the radome

⇧ Close-up on the forward portion of the FLIR

⇧ Looking at the rear contour of the FLIR

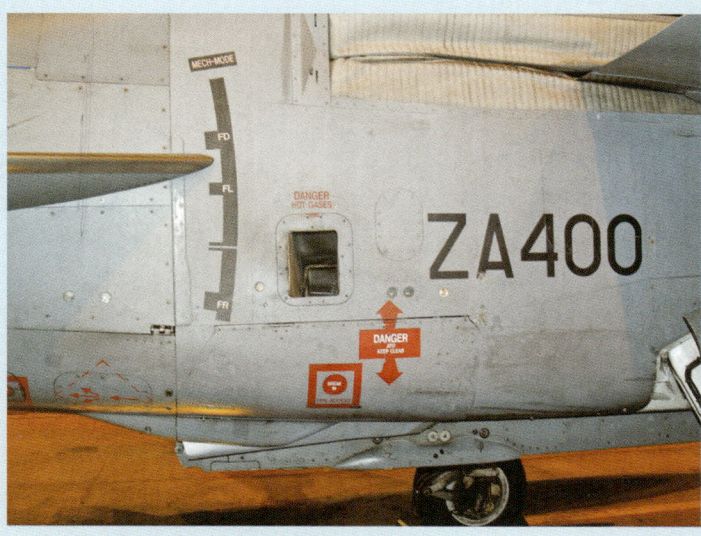

⇧ The access panel for the internal APU

⇧ The engine air intake

⇧ The Swedish BOL combined chaff launcher and Sidewinder missile rail

⇧ A plain Sidewinder missile rail on the inner face of the wing pylon

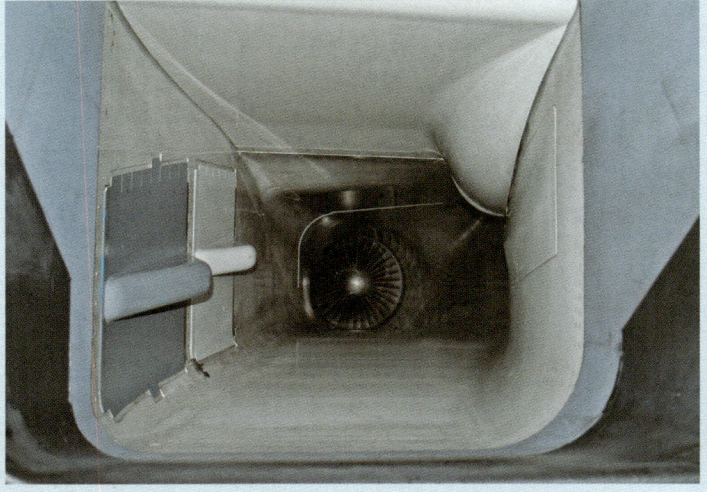

⇧ Straight down the engine intake – note the internal contours

⇧ Hot gas exhaust on the port underside

⇧ The tailplane joint

⇧ Close-in on the tailplane

⇧ The Tornado's twin engines in focus

⇧ Just above the afterburner cans are the thrust reverser buckets

⇧ Note the contour on the upper section of the BOZ pod where it meets the pylon

⇧ A BOZ-107 chaff and flare dispenser with faired-over rear section

⇧ A Marconi Sky Shadow ECM pod

⇧ The sharp nose of the BOZ-107 pod

⇧ The complex wing-slat arrangement

⇧ The IFR probe extended

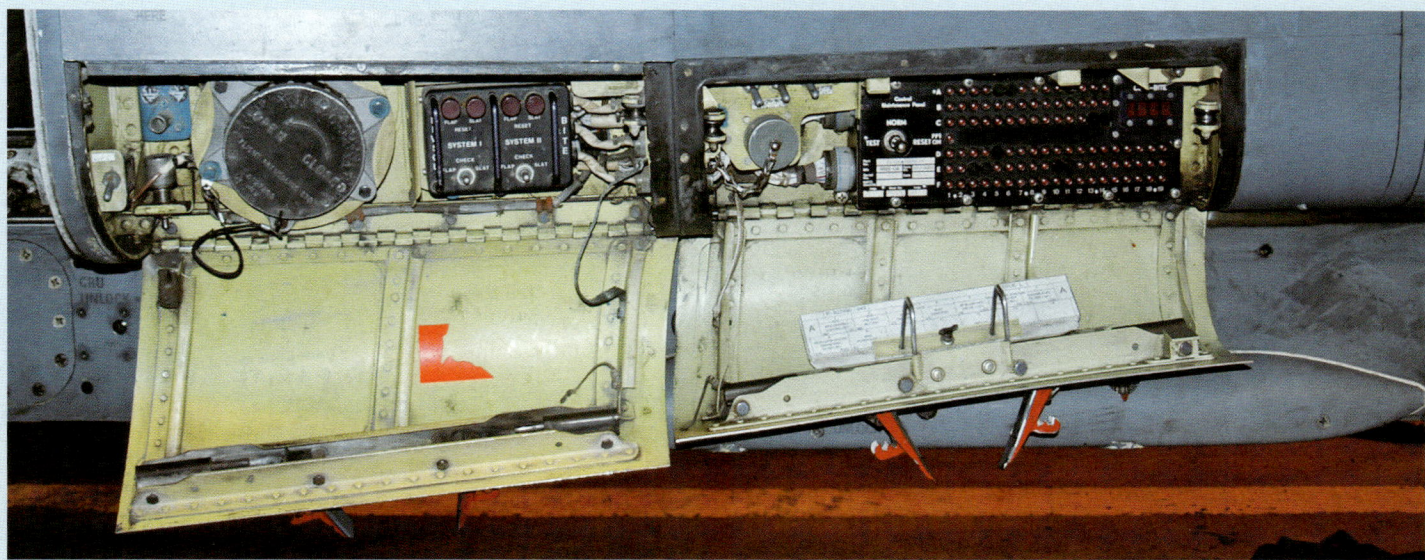
⇧ Fuel and ground management panel

⇧ Mainwheel leg and tyre

⇧ 'Red-Eye', complete with IFR probe in its housing

⇧ Mainwheel and wheel well

⇧ Looking upward into the nosewheel well

⇧ Inner face of one of the mainwheels

⇧ One of the twin airbrakes

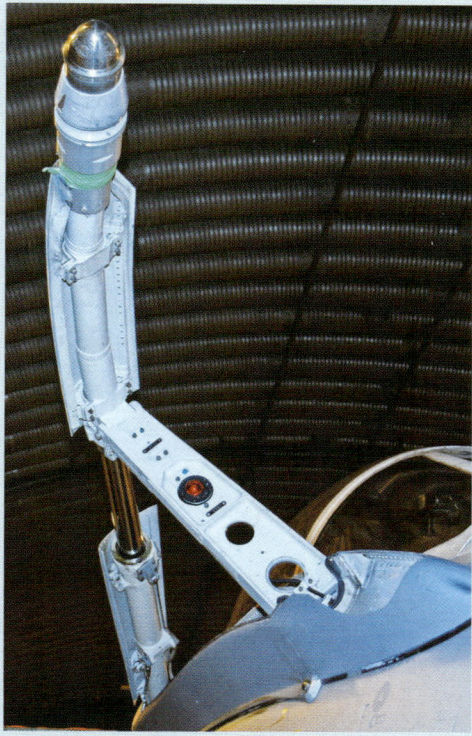

⇧ Note the 'bolt-on' nature of the IFR probe

⇧ GR.4 Front cockpit

⇧ GR.4 Rear cockpit

⇧ A grip fitted to the inner frame of navigator's station allows the firing of chaff and flares during high-g manoeuvres

⇧ Close-in on the Laser Ranger and Marked Target Seeker fairing

⇧ A CBLS (Carrier Bomb Light Stores) practice bomb carrier on the shoulder pylon

Chapter 6

Operation Granby

Desert Storm Tornadoes

Tornado GR.1/1A

For the Royal Air Force 'Desert Storm' the 1991 Gulf War came under the aegis of 'Operation Granby' their largest air operation since the recapture of the Falklands Islands nearly ten years earlier. 'Desert Sand' became the standard camouflage scheme, and in addition to some very high-tech weaponry dangling beneath the aircraft, many began to sport 'Nose-Art', a very traditional and personalised touch added by ground crews to provide a much needed lighter note to the conflict.

Numerically the Tornado represented 75% of the RAF's aircraft involved in Operation 'Granby' and during the course of the conflict a number of new items of kit were added to the aircraft's inventory, and indeed a new variant - the Tornado GR.1A - made its operational debut. An initial batch of Tornado GR.1s drawn from the assets of both RAF

⇧ ZD809/BA 'Awesome Annie' lands at the completion of another bombing raid

Germany and the UK were quickly despatched to the Gulf with RAF Bruggen being the first to send out twelve GR.1s to Muharraq in Bahrain on 27 August 1990, forming a composite unit. Crews for these aircraft came from Nos.IX, 15, 27, 31 and UK based 617 Squadron. A second composite Squadron came from RAF Germany's other Tornado base at Laarbruch, leaving for Muharraq on 19 September. Soon after arrival they were redeployed to Tabuk. Crews for this composite unit came from No.IX, 20, 14, 16, and 617 Squadrons. A third composite Squadron was also formed at Dhahran in early January 1991.

An Alkaline Removable Temporary Paint Finish (ARTF) called 'Desert Sand' was devised by the RAE in Farnborough and this involved spraying the whole airframe leaving the radome black and in some cases retaining the anti-glare panel atop the nose. The scheme extended to the pylons, wing-tanks and self-defence pods and was broken only by the natural metal areas around the Mauser cannon and engine exhausts Other modifications to the aircraft came under the umbrella of the 'Granby Phase 2 Updates', which included uprated RB.199 Mk 103 engines, making them more efficient in desert conditions. Radar Absorbent Material (RAM) was also added to the engine intakes and the leading edges of the wings, tailplanes and weapons

⇧ ZA447/EA MiG Eater surrounded by ground equipment

⇧ ZA469/I taxies out for another sortie

⇧ ZD792/CF 'Nursie' – note the weathered paintwork!

pylons, but was less apparent than on the Tornado F.3 as it was concealed beneath the Desert Sand colour. In all, some eight-four GR.1s were painted up for the Gulf, with some sixty being 'operational' during the hostilities. Initially the GR.1s were tasked with airfield denial using their JP233 dispensers, or 'toss bombing' 1,000lb bombs onto targets. As the JP233 had never been flown into combat before, the crews found that their sleek steeds 'flew like pigs' with these dispensers attached.

During the course of the hostilities, aside from their operational contribution, the Tornadoes received some very impressive personal paint jobs, in the form of really outrageous artwork that will for many remain the outstanding hallmark of the campaign. Most, but not all, featured some kind of scantily clad females in various states of undress. Some of the aircraft were given names that reflected their tail-codes such as ZD739/AC from Dhahran which became 'Armoured Charmer' and ZA491/N from Tabuk became 'Nikki'. Most artwork was painted on the port side of the nose, but again there were exceptions. Muharraq-based Tornadoes added a further touch by division into 'Snoopy Airways' and 'Triffid Airways'. Not to be outdone, Tabuk's aircraft all carried Sharkmouths to accompany their artwork. As the war progressed, the aircraft

⇧ ZD809/BA 'Awesome Annie' carrying two PGMs and 'Hindenburger' wing tanks

Operation Granby Tornadoes

Serial	Name
ZA392/EK	Lost 18/1/91
ZA396/GE	Lost 20/1/91
ZA399/GA	Zimmer Woman
ZA455/EJ	Triffid Airways
ZA456/M	Mel
ZA459/EL	
ZA463/Q	Flying High/Garfield
ZA469/I	
ZA471/E	Emma – Snoopy Airways
ZA472/EE	
ZA475/P	Triffid Airways
ZA491/N	Nikki – Snoopy Airways
ZA492/FE	
ZD717/C	Hello Kuwait Goodbye Iraq, Lost 14/1/91
ZD744BD	Birdstrike returned to Bruggen 18/1/91
ZD790/D	Debbie – Snoopy Airways
ZD791/BG	Lost 17/1/91
ZD850/CL	Cherry Lips
ZD851/AJ	Amanda Jane
ZD893/AG	Lost 20/1/03
ZA370/A	
ZA371/C	
ZA372/E	Sally T
ZA374/CN	Miss Behavin
ZA376	Mrs Miggins
ZA397/O	
ZA400/T	
ZA403/CO	Lost 23/1/03
ZA457/CE	Bob
ZA461/DK	
ZA490/GG	GiGi
ZD707/BK	
ZD715/DB	Luscious Lizzie
ZD719/AD	Check Six
ZD740/DA	Dhahran Annie
ZD745/BM	Black Magic
ZD843/DH	Damaged – returned to Bruggen 23/1/91
ZD841/CH	Where Do You Want It?
ZD895/BF	
ZD792/CF	Nursie
ZD809/BA	Awesome Annie
ZD890/O	
ZD892/H	Helen – Snoopy Airways
ZA393/CQ	Sir Gallahad
ZD406/DN	
ZA446/EF	
ZA447/EA	Mig Eater
ZA452/GK	Gulf Killer
ZA460/FD	Fire Dancer
ZA465/FK	Foxy Killer
ZA467/FF	Lost 22/1/03
ZA473/FM	Foxy Mama
ZA492/FE	
ZA719/AD	
ZA739/AC	Armoured Charmer
ZD744/BD	Buddha
ZD746/AB	Alarm Belle
ZD747/AL	Anna Louise
ZD748/AK	Anola Kay
ZD810/AA	
ZD844/DE	Donna Ewin
ZD845/AF	Angel Face
ZD848/BC	Bacardi & Coke

⇧ ZD745/BM 'Black Magic'

⇧ ZA460/FD 'Fire Dancer'

⇧ ZD719/AD 'Check Six'

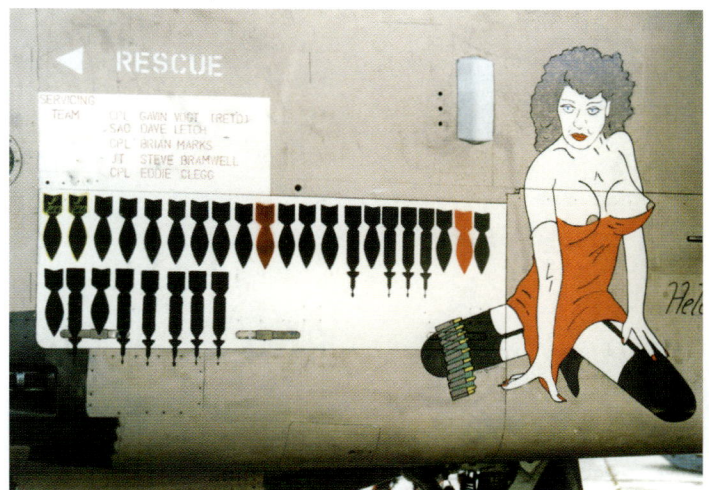
⇧ ZD892/H 'Helen'

⇧ ZA491/N 'Nikki'

⇧ ZD744/BD 'Buddha'

⇧ ZD850/CL 'Cherry Lips'

⇧ 'Snoopy Airways'

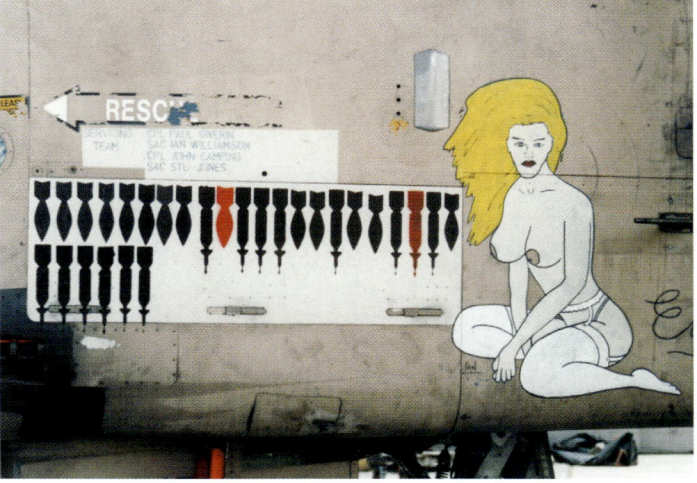
⇧ ZA471/E 'Emma'

also began to sport mission markings which reflected the ordnance carried These were generally applied to the port side of the fuselage, under the cockpit, and Muharraq-based aircraft had a panel specially painted to hold their mission symbols. The GR.1s also borrowed the larger 'Hindenburger' fuel tanks from their sister F.3s to give them a greater endurance, and to begin with these tanks retained the Air Defence Grey colour.

Tornado GR.1A

The new Tornado GR.1A 'recce-jets' operated by No.II (AC) Squadron and No.13 Squadron used video tape to record events, rather than the traditional 'wet film' process, and six GR.1As from No.II (AC) Squadron were readied for service in the Gulf. Each received the modifications adopted by all of the strike Tornadoes, and the recce software was quickly bought up to a higher standard and also, like the GR.1s, they borrowed the 460-gal 'Hindenburger' wing tanks from the F.3s. Since the GR.1As carried no offensive weaponry extra fuel could also be carried in two 330-gal tanks mounted on the under-fuselage shoulder stations.

The first GR.1A recce mission was mounted on the night of the 17 January, and was led by the OC of No.II (AC) Squadron, Squadron Leader Al Threadgould on a SCUD-hunt sortie. During the course of the early missions the first

⇧ A little 'bomb greeting'

⇧ One of the two TIALD pods sent to the Gulf nicknamed 'Sandra'

⇧ Happy New Year from Gazza's Gonads!

⇧ Who Ya Gonna Call – HAS Busters!

⇧ A JP233 is prepared for attachment

⇧ 'Debbie, Helen, Nikki and Emma' beneath their sun shelters!

image of a SCUD launcher was brought back by Squadron Leader Dick Garwood and Flt Lt Jon Hill, a recce crew from No.II (AC) Squadron flying ZA400, who were on a line-search sortie. Unlike the GR.1s, the GR.1As were more conservative in their approach to any sort of nose art-work or mission markings. Only one aircraft carried any sort of marking and that was ZA372/E, with the words 'Sally T' written on the port side of the nose. Tornado GR.1As flew some 128 recce missions, the longest being flown by Flt Lt Angus Hogg and Flt Lt Rick Haley which was of 4 hours 35 minutes duration, flying in ZA371. The GR.1A was particularly useful prior to the land war, when it undertook 'route searches' in areas earmarked for armoured columns to penetrate Iraq, providing vital information to planners and commanders.

TIALD

Rushed into service during the war was the GEC-Marconi TIALD gave the Tornado GR.1 the ability to provide a precision-aiming capability for aircraft using LGB's by day or night, and the system was so new that when Desert Storm began there were only two TIALD pods available and these were hurried to the Gulf. Five Tornado GR.1s were tasked with TIALD missions, and operated from Tabuk using crews from Nos.13 and 617 Squadrons. After a number of familiarisation flights the TIALD system was used operationally for the first time on 10 February, when ZD848/BC designated bombs for a four-ship attack on the H3 airfield in Iraq. The TIALD pod was mounted on the port 'shoulder' pylon, with a further 330-gallon tank mounted on the starboard shoulder pylon.

⇧ The impressive mission tally aboard ZD790/D 'Debbie'

ALARM

Like TIALD the ALARM missile system was still in the development stages and not yet released to Squadron service, and was again hastened into service. Based at Tabuk, the RAF employed nine aircraft in the ALARM role, eight from No.IX Squadron and one from No.17 Squadron. These aircraft went into the target area ahead of the main force to take out any radar defences, thus improving the

⇧ Note the kill mark aboard ZA492

survivability of the attacking aircraft. Initially configured to carry two missiles on the inboard wing pylons, replacing the tanks (overload fuel being carried on the underfuselage shoulder stations), a later mod saw them toting three ALARM's on launch rails on the shoulder and centreline pylons, the tanks returning to their underwing positions.

⇧ ZD715/DB 'Luscious Lizzie'

⇧ Coming home at dusk

Chapter 7
Tornadoes in 'Telic'

The 2003 Gulf War

On 6th February 2003 the UK Secretary of State for Defence announced Operation 'Telic' – the deployment of a force package comprising some 100-plus RAF aircraft to the Gulf region. This action was taken in response to the growing crisis over weapons of mass destruction within Iraq, and the demands of the United States, Great Britain, Spain and other countries that the Iraqi leadership should abide by United Nations Resolution 1441. The code word 'Telic' was derived from the Greek meaning 'purposeful', however one RAF quip explained that Telic stood for 'Tell Everyone Leave Is Cancelled'. The RAF's contribution to 'Gulf War II' was quoted as being a 'balanced and highly capable force'. The fixed wing aircraft involved included E-3D Sentry,

⇧ A second wave of Storm Shadow armed aircraft attacked targets just after dawn on the first day of the war

⇧ The new RAPTOR pod, another Telic debutante

Tornado GR.4/4A and F.3, Harrier GR.7, Canberra PR.9, VC10, Tri-Star, C-17 Globemaster and C-130 Hercules. ASRAAM armed Tornado F.3s provided air defence whilst Tornado GR.4s, and Harrier GR.7s provided the offensive and anti-radar capabilities, whist Storm Shadow cruise missiles and the RAPTOR reconnaissance pods made their operational debuts.

The Tornado GR.4 and GR.4A aircraft deployed to the Gulf came from units either based at Marham or RAF Lossiemouth. These aircraft left the UK on the 10th of February 2003 and were tasked to provide offensive air power as an Expeditionary Air Wing (EAW) which also comprised Rapid Reaction Force Elements. As well as the operational Tornado squadrons the EAW also maintained the Tactical IM-INT (Imagery Intelligence).

The upgraded Torrado GR.4/4A was a much more capable aircraft than the GR.1/1A used in the previous conflict and truly all-weather day- and night-capable with

⇧ A Tornado GR.4 armed with four ALARM anti-radar missiles taxies out

⇧ A Tornado GR.4 from No.617 Squadron armed with Storm Shadow cruise missiles is prepared for action on the first night of the conflict

⇧ A 'concrete bomb' designed for maximum impact, minimum collateral damage

⇧ A ground technician prepares a trio of ALARM missiles on this GR.4

⇧ One of the debutants in Telic was the Storm Shadow cruise missile

⇧ A deadly duo – TIALD and PGM

⇧ Shielded from the elements a GR.4 armed with PGMs is prepared for flight

Telic Tornado GR.4/GR.4A

GR.4

Code	Letter	Name	Payload
ZA449	AJ-N	Strathisla	9 Small LGB, 4 Bombs
ZA542	DM	Danger Mouse	
ZA547	DC		
ZA553	DI	Dishy Intel	
ZA554	BF	Born Fighter (Dennis the Menace & Gnasher Cartoon)	16 Small Lgb, 4 Storm Shadow
ZA559	AD	Aberlour	4 Small LGB, 1 Bomb
ZA560	BC	Benromach & Brave Coq (Foghorn Leghorn Cartoon)	9 Small LGB
ZA589	DN	Deadly Nightshade (Lady with Union Flag)	5 Storm Shadow, 6x ALARM 10x LGB
ZA592	BJ	Sharkmouth	9 LGB, 4 Dumb Bombs
ZA596	BL		
ZA600	AJ-L	Hot Stuff	7 Small LGB, 16 Large LGB, 4 Bombs, 3 ALARM, 6 Storm Shadow
ZA606	BD	Big Deal (Officer playing cards with Saddam)	4 ALARM, 14 LGB
ZA607	AB	Delightful Debs (We Are One, Coat Of Arms)	3 Alarm, 15 Black LGB, 2 Pink LGB
ZA611	TK		
ZA614	AJ-J	It's Show Time (Lady With Sunglasses Riding a Storm Shadow)	5 Storm Shadow, 4 Dumb Bombs, 15 LGB
ZD715	AM	Alarm Maiden/Here Comes (the) Sun	13 ALARM, 2 Large LGB, 15 Small LGB, 4 Concrete LGB
ZD720	TA	Talisker	6 Small LGB, 2 Large LGB, 4 Bombs & 4 ALARM
ZD740	DR	Desert Raven	5 LGB
ZD793	TB	Tamhdu	5 Small LGB
ZG714	Q	Truffle Snufflers & It's A Recce Thang (Scooby Doo & Daphne – Sharksmouth)	10 Small LGB, 4 Large LGB, 8 Alarm
ZG714	AJ-W	Johnnie Walker	3 ALARM, 8 LGB
ZG727	L	Look'n For Twouble (Elmer Fudd Cartoon)	7 Small LGB
ZG775	FB	Fat Boy	
ZG777	TC	Craigellachie	7 LGB
ZG792	AG-G		
ZG794	TF	Glenfarclas	5 LGB
ZG850	AJ-T	Rects Controllers Dream – The Glory Is In The Giving (Formerly Its Show Time I)	

GR.4A

Code	Letter	Name	Payload
ZG711	O	Oh Nell (Nell Mcandrew Caricature)	
ZG707	B	B.A.B.S	8 ALARM, 27 LGB
ZG726	K	Kylie	8 LGB
ZA394	G	The Grinch/Mean One	

⇧ ZA606/BD 'Big Deal'

⇧ ZG707 'BABS'

⇧ ZG727 'Look'n for Twouble'

⇧ ZD740 'Desert Raven'

⇧ ZA614 'It's Show Time'

⇧ ZA554 'Born Fighter'

its internal FLIR (Forward Looking Infra-Red) system complementing its already powerful radar and laser targeting systems. The GR.4s also carried the now mature TIALD (Thermal Image and Laser Designator) system on their under fuselage 'shoulder' pylons to allow the designation of laser guided precision weapons such as the Paveway II and III and Enhanced Paveway.

Another weapon in the Tornado's armoury was the ALARM anti-radiation missile, which made its combat debut in the 2001 Gulf War, used to attack Surface-to-Air Missile sites. Also new to the inventory was the Storm Shadow Cruise Missile, whilst a few new 'mods' were added to the Tornadoes for Gulf operations, especially in the cockpit, in the shape of 'sun shades' for the TV Tabs and the addition of two small joysticks attached to the canopy framing in the rear seat to help the Navigator to dispense chaff and flares whilst 'hanging on' during aggressive manoeuvres! Also a few Tornadoes were fitted with the Celcius Tech BOL chaff launchers.

The Tornado GR.4A 'Recce-Jet' provided tactical

⇧ Carrying Enhanced Paveway LGBs on the underfuselage shoulder stations ZD715/AM Alarm Maiden awaits the call to action

manufacturer to be covered in a grey synthetic coating and then refitted. These aircraft all wore toned-down roundels and fin-flashes with no sign of the garish 'Desert Pink' scheme from the 1991 conflict!

The crews and aircraft chosen for the initial Storm Shadow mission came from the Lossiemouth based No.617 Squadron, the famous 'Dambusters', who were taking part in 'an historic mission' on the 60th anniversary of the squadron's formation. The Storm Shadow missile was not

⇧ ZA553/DI 'Dishy Intel' armed with PGMs transits to its target area

reconnaissance using the TIRRS (Tornado Infra-Red Recce System), and the new RAPTOR pod which enhanced this capability to a real-time day and night scenario, with stand-off ranges of up to 50 miles. As well as being a specialist reconnaissance asset, the Tornado GR.4A also retained the full attack options of its GR.4 counterparts.

The Tornado GR.4s sported a new ARTF (Alkaline Removable Temporary Finish) light-grey overall finish and this included a darker grey radome with white serials and white codes. This was then changed to a white serial with grey codes. Sources indicate that the radomes were not actually painted but removed and returned to the

due to enter service until later that year, although the squadron had been running test flights with dummies. In addition to the high-tech laser-guided GPS-aided Paveway III bombs carried by the Tornado, consideration was given to using weapons at the other end of the spectrum. Far removed from the £750,000-each Storm Shadow rounds, came the most extreme use of precision-guided inert munitions so far recorded. These weapons are basically

⇧ ZA592 and an impressive sharksmouth

⇧ A 'Telic Tonka' taxies out

⇧ ZG725 'Kylie'

⇧ ZA542/DM 'Danger Mouse'

⇧ ZG850 'The glory is in the giving'

blocks of concrete shaped as bombs and painted blue to identify them as non-explosive if they are discovered still intact after the war! Albeit they were to be laser-guided 1,000lb blocks of concrete! Each was capable of destroying a tank or artillery piece, but without causing a devastating explosion that would put civilians at risk and shatter surrounding buildings.

⇧ ZA607/AB 'Delightful Debs' returns to base carrying a RAPTOR recce pod at the end of an intel mission

⇧ Armourers prepare a brace of Enhanced Paveway PGMs slung under this GR.4

Like in the first Gulf War, artwork was applied to most of the combat aircraft involved. The Tornado GR.4/4As, having numerically the lion's share of UK aircraft, carried the most artwork. Every attempt was made to mimic the tail code of the aircraft with the theme or initials of the artwork, and female figures were avoided, or at least clothed, in case the aircraft had to divert to Saudi Arabia – Moslem sensitivities were to be respected. Cartoon characters were a favourite amongst the budding artists, although 617 Squadron machines were simply named after brands of Scottish Whiskey. One aircraft ZG850 was used as a source of spares until finally repaired, and was thus painted with a Christmas tree artwork with the logo – 'The glory is in the giving'.

Chapter 8

Luftwaffe IDS

⇧ 43+64 in the grey and white scheme of the Marineflieger Tornadoes

The first service delivery of the Luftwaffe's Tornado IDS was made on 27 July 1979 followed by a further 247 IDS variants, including 35 special ECRs. Originally the Tornadoes equipped five fighter-bomber wings, replacing the F-104 Starfighter. Two wings were disbanded in 2003 and 2005 and a third was re-equipped with the Tornado ECR. In addition to the order made by the Luftwaffe, the German Navy's Marineflieger also received 112 IDS variants These equipped two wings until 1994, when MFG1 was disbanded followed by MFG2 in 2005 with its aircraft and duties being passed on to the Luftwaffe, whilst also forming up a new reconnaissance wing as described separately.

Beginning in 2000 German IDS, ECR and Reconnaissance

⇧ The fearsome MWI dispenser carried beneath a German IDS

⇧ 43+62 of MFG1

⇧ 43+01 of 'B' Flight within the TTTE

⇧ Seen in the early Luftwaffe scheme of Black, Yellow Olive, Basalt Grey and Silver, G-34 of the 'Standards' flight at the TTTE taxies out

⇧ Firing out its bomblets, the MW-1 served a similar purpose to that of the RAF's JP-233

⇧ 98+60 one of the MRCA prototypes makes a colourful departure

⇧ An MFG1 Tornado with 'buddy-buddy' refuelling pack on the centreline

⇧ 43+65 showing nosewheel depression as the thrust reverser buckets slow the aircraft down

⇧ The Rafael Litening II Laser Designator pod

⇧ Rafael Litening II pod and associated GBU-24 Paveway II PGM

⇧ Big Orange Nose – Panavia Tornado PA-200 of WTD 61

⇧ A superb rendering of an eagle's-eye

⇧ Nose section of the Tornado housing the TFR system

⇧ The Luftwaffe use the Boz-103 chaff and flare dispenser pod

⇧ Forward fuselage of WTD 61

⇧ The complex wing-slat arrangement of the Tornado IDS

⇧ Tail markings of WTD 61

⇧ The wing-mounted TSPJ electronic jammer

⇧ Close-in on the superb tail art

⇧ Tail marking of JG33

⇧ Tail marking of AG51

⇧ Tail marking

⇧ Tail marking of JG31 'Boelke'

⇧ Tail marking of JG32

⇧ G-70 in later camouflage, also of 'Standards' flight within the TTTE

⇧ Head-on view of a Tornado IDS with Rafael Litening II pod and associated GBU-24 Paveway II PGM

⇧ A JG33 Tornado powers away. Note the Litening II pod on the shoulder station

⇧ 50 years!

⇧ Tornado training is undertaken at Holloman AFB in New Mexico and here an IDS is seen high over the plains

⇧ 45+94 outside its HAS

⇧ 45+88 of JG33 carrying an inert Taurus Cruise Missile

⇧ Note the very sooty tail, a Tornado trait

⇧ A fantastic scheme celebrating 50 years of JB33 from the right...

⇧ ...and from the left

Tornados all received the ASSTA 1 (Avionics System Software Tornado in Ada) upgrade. This involved the replacement of the weapons computer with a MIL-STD 1553/1760 or Ada MIL-STD 1815 computer. The Tornadoes also received an internal GPS, a Laser INS, and the Tornado Self Protection Jammer ECM-pod. Due to the new computer uprated HARM and Kormoran II missiles could be carried as could the Rafael Litening II Laser Designator pod and GBU-24 Paveway II bombs and furthermore the aircraft is planned to carry the new IRIS-T infrared-guided air-to-air missile, being developed by BGT. The ASSTA 2 upgrade began in 2005 only for the 85 ECR and RECCE Tornados, as the IDS is in the process of being replaced by the Eurofighter Typhoon and this upgrade consists mainly of digital avionics, a new ECM suite and the new Taurus Cruise Missile.

German Tornadoes undertook NATO combat operations during the war in the Balkans, which saw the first combat operation for the Luftwaffe since World War II alongside British and Italian IDS aircrafts also participating. In 2007, a detachment of 6 Tornadoes of AG-51 also deployed to Mazar-i-Sharif in Northern Afghanistan to support NATO forces.

⇧ Another astonishing scheme – here from JG33

Chapter 9

Luftwaffe ECR

During the early 1980s the German Air Force was searching for an aircraft that could not only supplement the other Luftwaffe reconnaissance aircraft like the RF-4E but also offer the ability for SEAD (Suppression of Enemy Air Defences) using the Texas Instruments AGM-88 HARM. The Tornado was selected as the basis to meet this need and thirty-five aircraft were ordered with two development aircraft being converted from existing IDS airframes to prove the concept. The first production aircraft made its first flight on 26 October 1989 and deliveries began in May 1990. At the heart of the ECR Tornado's abilities is the ELS – Emitter Location System (although initially thirty aircraft did not have the ELS fitted, thus relied on their RHWR and the HARM seeker heads for acquisition data until the system was retro-fitted to all aircraft) allowing the accurate mapping of ground radar threats and the ability to launch missiles against them, and to back this up with secondary reconnaissance ability. The ECR differs from the standard IDS by the addition of an underfuselage teardrop recce fairing like that of the RAF Tornado GR.1A and an antenna adjacent to the nosewheel

⇧ Looking decidedly mucky, 46+54 in the newer grey colours carries HARM, Sidewinder and ECM pod

door containing a Carl-Zeiss steerable FLIR and the deletion of the Mauser cannon, the space being taken up by the ELS equipment. As the fundamental role of the Luftwaffe ECR Tornado is that of a pathfinder, the aircraft came equipped with the LITEF ODIN, a digital data-link for transmission of near-real-time reconnaissance data to following aircraft and ground centres. The FLIR adds to the aircraft's already impressive low-level abilities in adverse weather conditions

⇧ Hooked up to the tanker. Note the contours of the bolt-on IFR probe as it meets the fuselage

⇧ 46+44 specially painted for the 2002 Tiger Meet and wearing a most striking scheme showing the standard camouflage scheme peeling back to reveal the Tiger striping underneath

⇧ 46+48 in another variation of the 'Tiger Theme'

⇧ ECR and reconnaissance Tornadoes flew the Luftwaffe's first combat missions since 1945 when they took part in NATO's Operation 'Deny Flight'

⇧ 44+14 prepares to take on fuel from a USAF tanker. Note the earlier three-tone camouflage and the dark and light grey wing tanks

⇧ Note the green BOZ-103 pod on this ECR

⇧ The port side of 46+23 which celebrates 50 years of JaboG 32 in some style

⇧ A Tornado tail – this one being from JG-51

⇧ BOZ-103 Chaff and flare dispenser pod

⇧ The teeth of the ECR, the HARM missile

⇧ Note the finlets applied to the rear of the TSPJ electronic jammer pod

⇧ **Spot the difference... the starboard side of 46+23!**

⇧ **...the port side**

and at night. However building on the lessons from the campaign over Bosnia all ECR Tornadoes have now been reconfigured as a pure SEAD platform deleting all reconnaissance equipment.

The key features of the Tornado ECR are:
• Raytheon Emitter Location System (ELS)
• Northrop Grumman/EADS Company Enhanced Radar Warning Equipment (ERWE) II system
• SaabTech (formerly CelsiusTech) BOZ 101 Counter Measures Dispensing System (CMDS) pod
• EADS/Elta Tornado Self-Protection Jammer (TSPJ)
• Raytheon Ku-band ground-mapping and terrain-following radar
• A BAE Systems Avionics FIN 1010 three-axis digital Inertial Navigation System (INS)
• LITEF Spirit series central mission computer
• Microtecnica air-data computer
• LITEF Operational Data INterface (ODIN) data link system
• Rohde & Schwarz XD610H1 'Have Quick II' compatible communications transceiver
• Siemens STR 700 identification friend-or-foe transponder
• Thales Communications TACAN system
• Raytheon instrument landing system
• NATO (MIL-STD) 1553B databus

All this equipment makes the ECR Tornado to the most capable dedicated SEAD aircraft in service, since retirement of the USAF F-4G Wild Weasel. ECR and reconnaissance Tornadoes flew the Luftwaffe's first combat missions since 1945 when they took part in NATO's Operation 'Deny Flight'. EG 1 flew the first mission over Bosnia on 31 August 1995 and remained in Italy until 22 November 1995. It flew around 800 sorties but fired no HARMs 'in anger'. The ECRs also played an important role in Operation 'Allied Force' and again EG 1 launched its first SEAD mission on the night of 24 March 1999. Its ECR Tornadoes remained in theatre until 2 July 1999 and during that time the ECR Tornadoes had flown over 400 SEAD combat missions and fired some 236 HARM missiles against air defence targets. The ECR force also found out that it was better to operate their mission in pairs as a single aircraft offered only a low kill-ratio whereas a brace of aircraft had a greater effect in triangulating hostile emitter locations. As part of the The ASSTA 2 (Avionics System Software Tornado in Ada) upgrade which began in 2005 the ECR Tornados are in the process of being upgraded with new digital avionics, a new ECM suite and the equipment to carry the Taurus Cruise Missile.

Luftwaffe ECR Tornado
Walkaround

Pictures by Michael Ullman

⇧ Looking upwards at the windshield

⇧ Nose-mounted pitot tube

⇧ Open access panel on the port side of the nose. Note the 'Armament' stencil above the panel door

⇧ Looking up inside the canopy

⇧ Port intake and associated light

⇧ Looking along the wing/fuselage joint. Note the black aerial for the Emitter Locator System

⇧ Under the fuselage is the small fairing containing the Carl-Zeiss steerable FLIR

⇧ Port side inner wing pylon and fuel tank

⇧ Port side outer wing pylon

⇧ Two HARM missiles mounted on the 'shoulder' stations

⇧ Close-in on the nosewheel struts

⇧ Head-on at the nosewheels and landing gear

⇧ Nosewheels viewed from the port side

⇧ Looking upward at the runway arrestor hook

⇧ Looking at the rear fuselage; of note is the wing sweep bag, and the incidence marker for the tailplane

⇧ Looking upwards at the engine access panels

⇑ Located between the engine nozzles are the gears that operate the thrust reverser 'buckets'

⇑ Straight inside the afterburner can

⇑ A rather soot-stained tail

⇑ Starboard side pylon and wing

⇑ Fuel tank and dummy Sidewinder missile

⇑ The inner face of one of the mainwheels

⇑ Main wheel outer face

⇑ The mainwheel head-on

⇧ Looking up under the starboard wingtip

⇧ The ground service and refuelling panel

⇧ Hydraulic pressure gauges

⇧ Close-in on the IFR probe in its cradle

⇧ The starboard ELS antennae

⇧ Liquid oxygen bottle in its open panel

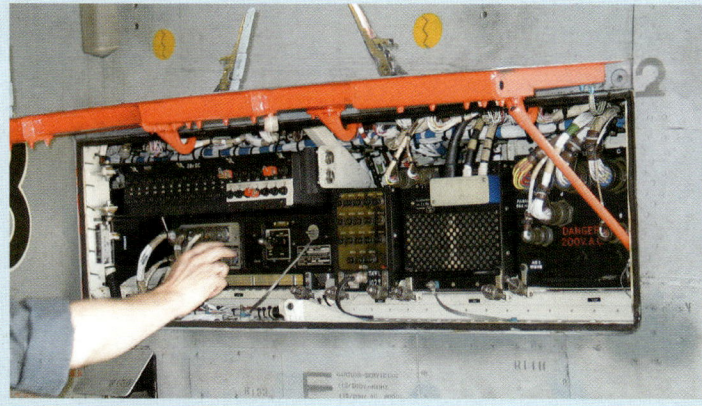
⇧ Port side electronics panel open

⇧ Starboard side of the nose showing the 'bolt-on' IFR probe

Chapter 10

Luftwaffe Recon

As noted in the section on the ECR Tornado the 'reconnaissance' element of the aircraft's role was dropped from the Luftwaffe aircraft's profile, however this was later revived with the transfer of a number of ex-Marineflieger recce aircraft to the Luftwaffe in the mid-1990s. These former naval aircraft now make up the equipment of the dedicated Luftwaffe reconnaissance squadron AG51 which subsequently adopted the unit markings of AG52 with a small change to the number its badge was reflecting.

⇧ 46+20 with the GAF-Recce Pod

DB/Aeritalia Pod

The AG51 aircraft were initially equipped with underfuselage-mounted DB/Aeritalia pods housing two Zeiss cameras and a Texas Instruments RS-710 IRLS, inherited from the Marineflieger. This made them less capable than the Phantoms they replaced. This pod contained twin Zeiss film cameras and an infrared line scanner (IRLS). The IRLS was sensitive enough to detect freshly disturbed earth (useful for both landmines and arms caches). The Tornadoes of AG51 are armed only for self-defence with drop-tanks, countermeasures pods and Sidewinder AAMs.

Telelens Pod

Similar to the recce pod, the Telelens pod is equipped with three camera positions. The front section of the recce pod is modified and its external structure extended to accommodate a Telelens camera with a long focal length. In addition to the Telelens camera in the front position, which

GAF-Recce-Pod

The DB/Aeritalia system was replaced by a more sophisticated GAF-Recce-Pod, however they use conventional 'wet film' cameras. The reconnaissance pod is mounted to the centreline pylon of Tornadoes belonging to AG51 'Immelmann' which has some thirty of these pods at its disposal which come in two different variants. Each variant is equipped with two optical cameras and one infrared line-scanner (infrared sensor) which can be adapted to the individual mission profile in a modular manner.

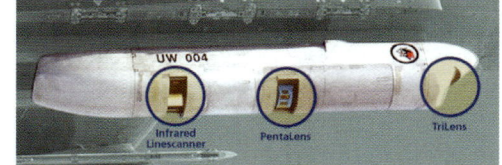

⇧ Elements of the GAF-Recce Pod

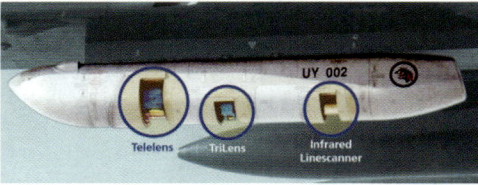

⇧ Elements of the Telelens Pod

can be panned perpendicular to the direction of flight, either a tri-lens camera or a penta-lens camera can be installed in the centre position. The third position is used in both reconnaissance pods for installation of the infrared line scanner.

⇧ One of the ex-Marineflieger Tornadoes now with AG51

⇧ The AG51 aircraft were initially equipped with underfuselage-mounted DB/Aeritalia pods

⇧ Telelens pod left side

⇧ Telelens Pod right side

⇧ 45+57 with the Telelens Pod

⇧ Note the camouflage differences here on these two GAF – Pod-equipped Tornadoes

Chapter 11

Italian Tornado IDS

The Italian Air Force, the Aeronautica Militaire Italia, had set its requirement at 100 Tornado IDS. The first of the AMI's aircraft was pre-series airframe X-588, and this was followed by ninety-nine from subsequent production batches. Unusually, Italy assigns separate serial blocks to its dual-control aircraft, even though they retain full combat capabilities. After X-588 had been renumbered MM7001, the first production IDS emerged as MM7002 to 7008, and the twin-stick aircraft as MM55000 to MM55011. Deliveries to AMI units began on 3 March 1981, when MM7001 was flown to Pratica di Mare to be used by the Reparto Sperimentale Volo (RSV) (Experimental Flight Department) and received the code RS-10. The second production aircraft, MM7003, was temporarily assigned for maintenance familiarisation and was delivered to Camerai-Novara on 17 April 1982 to allow the 1° Centro Manutenzione Principale to prepare for its task of training ground personnel to undertake level-three overhauls and repairs. Of the 100 Tornadoes bought by the AMI, originally only fifty-four were assigned to front-line units, the remaining thirty-six being held in reserve or placed with the TTTE at RAF Cottesmore.

⇧ **Italian Tornadoes share a large proportion of their combat equipment with their German counterparts**

Italian Tornadoes share a large proportion of their combat equipment with their German counterparts. Self-defence equipment beneath the wings comprises a Philips BOZ-100 chaff/flare dispenser, AEG Cerberus II jamming pod and AIM-9L Sidewinder AAMs. Offensive armament can include the MW-1 dispenser, of which 100 had been purchased along with the AGM-65D Maverick and MBB Kormoran AShMs for the anti-shipping role. The MBB-Aeritalia centreline reconnaissance pod is also used for imagery by traditional, TV and infra-red linescan means. The bolt-on IFR probe was used by Italian Tornadoes during the Gulf War and also when taking part in overseas exercises. A further order was placed for a number of ECR Tornadoes (see separate section). The AMI Tornadoes have undergone an upgrade programme which included the SMS90 stores management system enabling the aircraft to deliver PGMs, and the AMI also purchased the Thomson Convertible Laser Designation Pod (CLDP) with both TV and IR capabilities for use with Paveway bombs.

The Italian Air Force also operates Kormoran-equipped Tornado IDS in the anti-shipping role and their main tasking is that of maritime-strike protecting Italy's shipping lanes. Italian Tornadoes undertook low-level flypasts over Serbian shipping during Operation Sharp Guard above the Adriatic

⇧ **A trio of grey-clad Italian IDS**

⇧ **Wearing the more familiar Italian colours MM7058/6-60 is towed back to the flight-line**

⇧ Note the ELS antenna by the nosewheel door, and plenty of exposed panels

⇧ Close-up on the nose section; note the lack of a reconnaissance fairing

⇧ The intricate tail art aboard MM7027

⇧ Close-in detail of the nose section

⇧ Note the bolt-in IFR probe slightly open on this ECR

⇧ An Italian ECR taxies in

Chapter 13

Saudi Tornadoes

Saudi Arabia remains the sole 'export' customer for Tornado. In September 1985, the massive £4,000 million Al Yamamah I – 'Bird of Peace' – deal was signed by the Saudi and UK governments, covering forty-eight IDS and twenty-four ADV Tornados, along with thirty Hawks, two radar-training Jetstreams and thirty BAe-built Pilatus PC-9s. Saudi Arabia had previously bought BAC Strikemasters and Lightnings, but was far more used to buying US equipment, to which their massive fleet of F-15s bears witness. The Tornado faced stiff competition from the F-15E which was oddly

⇧ Note the canopy is shielded from the desert sun

⇧ Close-in on the Saudi insignia

forced to struggle against some strange constraints, including a US refusal to supply conformal fuel tanks or multiple ejector racks - something prompted by the Israeli government - and a further demand that the aircraft could not be based at Tabuk, the most northern Saudi airfield, which most threatened Israel. In the end, though, the attack-configured F-15 was seen to be too much of an unknown quantity, and as the Tornado IDS had already reached a level of proven maturity, the British option looked the more attractive. Saudi aircrew flew Tornado evaluation sorties from RAF Honington in 1984 and the arms deal was announced the following year.

Once Saudi Arabia had signed for the Tornado it wanted early deliveries, so eighteen RAF GR.1s and two German IDSs were diverted to the RSAF from Batch 5 orders, and all twenty-four ADVs were diverted from the RAF's Batch 6 with some RAF places at TTTE also being given to Saudi crews, who began training there in October 1985. Deliveries to 7 Squadron RSAF (formerly operators of the Northrop F-5E) at Dhahran began with 701-704 (ex-ZD997, ZD998, ZE114 and ZE115) on 26 and 27 March 1986 and was followed by 705 and 706 in April. Trainers were 704 to 706, 759, 768 and 769, of which the two last-mentioned were scratch-built by BAe. The remaining twenty-eight IDS aircraft were built from Batch 7 and these began appearing in the February of 1988. These aircraft now had the optional bolt-on retractable in-

⇧ 'Everything down' as this Saudi IDS comes in to land

⇧ Saudi aircraft have the optional bolt-on retractable in-flight refueling probe and were reportedly delivered with Sea Eagle missiles, JP233 and were ALARM capable

⇧ The Saudi Tornadoes are the most colourful currently flying

⇧ A pair of Saudi Tornadoes on a pre-delivery flight

⇧ With a practice bomb carrier attached to the shoulder pylon this Saudi IDS waits under its 'sun shelter'

also took part in the 1991 Gulf War, flying operational profiles similar to that of their RAF and Italian counterparts.

In September 2006, BAe Systems was awarded a contract to upgrade eighty Saudi Tornadoes.

Saudi Tornado Colours

The Saudi Tornado IDSs are the most colourful of all the operational aircraft with their three-tone desert scheme of Light Stone BS381 C361, Dark Earth BS381 C450 and Dark Green BS381 C649.

flight refueling probe and were reportedly delivered with Sea Eagle missiles, JP233 and were ALARM capable. Furthermore the last six aircraft delivered were of the GR.1A reconnaissance standard and had the RAF-style fin fuel tank incorporated into their design. The aircraft also received SWAM (Surface Wave Absorbent Material) on the leading edges of the fin, wings and tailplanes, and (RAM Absorbent Material) tiles applied to the engine intake area, necessitating the removal of the engines to allow them to be bonded to the intakes adjacent to the first stage of the fan. Al Yamamah II, agreed on 1 July 1988, originally covered a further twelve IDS and thirty-six ADVs; however, the contract was cancelled in July 1990, and subsequently amended to total forty-eight of the IDS version. The Saudi Tornadoes

⇧ Close-up of the Saudi tail markings

Appendix

Charts

Tornado Development History

MRCA
Original designation for Tornado programme, meaning Multi-Role Combat Aircraft.

Tornado prototypes
Initial development batch of nine aircraft.

Tornado pre-series
Follow-on development batch of 6 aircraft.

Tornado IDS
Generic term for 'bomber' version. IDS – Interdictor/Strike.

Tornado ADV
Generic term for dedicated interceptor fighter version. Described separately.

Tornado GR.1
Standard strike version of the Tornado IDS for the RAF. Features additional fin fuel tank and laser rangefinder in under nose fairing.

Tornado GR.1(T)
Version of the Tornado GR1 with full flying controls in both cockpits for pilot training. Fifty aircraft plus one pre-series refurbished.

Tornado GR.1A
Dedicated reconnaissance version of GR.1. Includes Vinten 4000 infra-red line-scan video system in blister fairing below the aircraft nose. Fourteen aircraft new build plus sixteen conversions.

Tornado GR.1B
Dedicated anti-shipping version of GR.1. Equipped to launch Sea Eagle missiles and carry 'buddy' in-flight refuelling pods.

Tornado GR.4
Mid-Life Update for GR.1 with upgraded avionics and cockpit systems.

Tornado GR.4A
Mid-Life Update for GR.1A with upgraded avionics and cockpit systems

Tornado IDS Germany
Version of Tornado IDS for Germany. Features different weapons ejector racks and weapons fit. 212 aircraft for Luftwaffe (including two refurbished pre-series and fifty dual control). 112 aircraft for Navy.

Tornado IDS Italy
Version of Tornado IDS for the Italian Air Force. Very similar to German version. 100 aircraft (including one refurbished pre-series and twelve dual-control).

Tornado IDS Saudi
Export version of Tornado IDS for the Royal Saudi Air Force. Very similar to RAF GR.1 version. Ninety-six aircraft (including fourteen dual-control and six reconnaissance versions similar to GR.1A).

Tornado ECR
Version of Tornado IDS dedicated to reconnaissance and enemy air defence suppression. Only Tornados with RB.199 Mk 105 engines. Thirty-five aircraft new-build for Germany, sixteen aircraft conversions for Italy.

Tornado Build

British Aerospace

Version	Quantity	Assembly Location	Time Period
Tornado prototypes	4	Warton	March 1973-1976
Tornado pre-series	3	Warton	1976-1978
Tornado GR.1	228	Warton	1978-1985
Tornado GR.1A	16	Warton	1985-1989
Tornado GR.1A	14	Warton	1989-1993
Tornado IDS Saudi	48	Warton	1986-1993
Tornado IDS Saudi	48	Warton	1993-1999
Tornado GR.4/4A	142	Warton	1997-2002
Total:	**345**		

MBB

Version	Quantity	Assembly Location	Time Period
Tornado prototypes	4	Manching	1974-1977
Tornado pre-series	2	Manching	1977-1978
Tornado IDS	322	Manching	1979-1990
Tornado ECR	35	Manching	1990-Jan 1992
Total:	**363**		

Alenia

Version	Quantity	Assembly Location	Time Period
Tornado prototypes	1	Turin	1975-1975
Tornado pre-series	1	Turin	1977-1978
Tornado IDS	99	Turin	1981-1990
Tornado ECR	16	Turin	1992-1994
Total:	**101**		

⇧ **ZG729/M in Arctic camouflage applied for a visit to Norway**

Tornado Operators

AMI

Unit	Base	Version	Status	Notes
102° Gruppo, 6° Stormo		Ghedi	IDS	Active
154° Gruppo, 6° Stormo		Ghedi	IDS	Active
156° Gruppo C.B., 36° Stormo	Gioia del Colle	IDS	Inactive	
155° Gruppo E.T.S., 50° Stormo	San Damiano	ECR	Active	
53° Stormo		Cameri	ECR	Inactive

German Navy

Unit	Base	Version	Status	Notes
Marinefliegergeschwader 1	Jagel		Disbanded	1982-1993
Marinefliegergeschwader 2	Eggebek		Disbanded	1986-2005

Luftwaffe

Unit	Base	Version	Status	Notes
Jagdbombergeschwader 31 'Boelcke'	Nörvenich	IDS	Active	
Jagdbombergeschwader 32	Lagerlechfeld	ECR	Active	
Jagdbombergeschwader 33	Büchel	IDS	Active	
Jagdbombergeschwader 34 'Allgäu'	Memmingen		Disbanded	Disbanded 2003
Jagdbombergeschwader 38 'Friesland'	Jever		Disbanded	Disbanded 2005
Aufklärungsgeschwader 51 'Immelmann'	Jagel/Schleswig	IDS	Active	

RAF

Unit	Base	Version	Status	Notes
No.2 Squadron	Marham	GR.4/4A	Active	12 aircraft
No.9 Squadron	Marham	GR.4/4A	Active	12 aircraft
No.11 Squadron	Leeming	F.3	Disbanded	1988-2005
No.12 Squadron	Lossiemouth	GR.4/4A	Active	12 aircraft
No.13 Squadron	Marham	GR.4/4A	Active	12 aircraft
No.14 Squadron	Lossiemouth	GR.4/4A	Active	12 aircraft
No.XV (Reserve) Squadron	Lossiemouth	GR.4	Reserve	26 aircraft. GR4 OCU
No.16 Squadron	Laarbruch	GR.1	Disbanded	1983-1991
No.17 Squadron	Brüggen	GR.1	Disbanded	1985-1999
No.20 Squadron	Laarbruch	GR.1	Disbanded	1984-1992
No.27 Squadron	Marham	GR.1	Disbanded	1983-1993
No.29 Squadron	Coningsby	F.3	Disbanded	1987-1998
No.31 Squadron	Marham	GR.4/4A	Active	12 aircraft
Tri-National Tornado Training Establishment	Cottesmore	IDS, GR.1	Disbanded	
Tornado WCU (No.45 Squadron)	Honington	GR.1	Renumbered XV(R)	1981-1992

Royal Saudi Air Force

Unit	Base	Version	Status	Notes
No.7 Squadron RSAF		IDS		
No.29 Squadron RSAF		ADV		
No.34 Squadron RSAF		ADV		
No.66 Squadron RSAF		IDS		
No.75 Squadron RSAF		IDS		
No.83 Squadron RSAF		IDS		

⇓ Tornado ECR 50-43 of 50 Stormo Italian Air Force finished in overall Light Grey. Note the lack of the reconnaissance fairing under the forward fuselage

⇓ Tornado IDS 36-52 of 156 Gruppo, 36 Stormo Italian Air Force finished in Grey FS36820 and Green FS34079 disruptive upper surfaces and Aluminium FS37178 lower surfaces

⇓ Tornado IDS '67' in its 'Operation Locusta' colours as worn during Operation Desert Storm in 1991. This consists of Sand Yellow FS33448 upper surfaces and Aluminium FS37178 lower surfaces. The aircraft is heavily weathered due to its exposure to the elements in the Gulf

⇓ Tornado GR.1 of No.IX Squadron RAF in a two-tone wraparound scheme of standard Dark Sea Grey BS381C: 638 and Dark Green BSC381C: 641

⇓ Tornado GR.1A ZG729/M of No.13 Squadron RAF wearing a temporary water-soluble white paint over the grey portion of the standard RAF Grey/Green wraparound scheme for a cold weather exercise in northern Norway

⇩ Tornado GR.1 ZA465/FD 'Fire Dancer' as seen during Operation Granby, the RAF's contribution to Operation Desert Storm in 1991. The aircraft wears and overall ARTF finish of 'Desert Sand'

⇩ Tornado GR.4 ZA591/058 of No.31 Squadron RAF wearing a two-tone camouflage scheme of Dark Sea Grey BS381C: 638 upper surfaces and Dark Camouflage Grey BS381C: 626 on the fuselage sides and lower surfaces

⇩ Tornado GR.4 ZA614/AJJ 'It's Show Time' of No.617 Squadron RAF as seen during Operation Telic 2003 and finished in overall Camouflage Grey BS381C: 626 ARTF

⇩ Tornado GR.4 ZD720/086 of No.14 Squadron RAF finished in overall BS381C: 626 Dark Camouflage Grey

⇩ Tornado IDS 43+54 of Marineflieger Geschwader 1 (MFG1) of the German Navy and finished on Grey RAL 7012 upper surfaces and White RAL 7035 lower surfaces

⇩ Tornado IDS 46+11 of Marineflieger Geschwader 1 (MFG1) of the German Navy finished in the Marine Standard F scheme of RAL 5008, RAL 7009 and RAL 7012 disruptive

⇩ Tornado IDS 45+76 of JBG38 'Friesland', and finished Luftwaffe Standard C scheme of RAL 7021, RAL6003 and FS 34079 disruptive

⇩ Tornado IDS 45+44 of JBG33 and finished in a Luftwaffe Standard 1995 scheme of FS36375, FS36320 and FS35237 disruptive

⇩ Tornado ECR 45+51 of AG51 'Immelmann' finished in a scheme of FS36375, FS36320 and FS35237 disruptive

⇩ Tornado IDS 6612 converted to GR.4 Standard of the Royal Saudi Air Force and finished in BS381C: 361 Light Stone, BS381C: 450 Dark Earth and BS381C: 649 Dark Green disruptive